Family Prayers
for
Daily Grace

Renee Bartkowski

Liguori
ONE LIGUORI DRIVE
LIGUORI MO 63057-9999

Imprimi Potest:
Richard Thibodeau, C.Ss.R.
Provincial, Denver Province
The Redemptorists

ISBN 0-7648-0962-8
Library of Congress Catalog Card Number: 2002106821

To order, call 1-800-325-9521
www.liguori.org
www.catholicbooksonline.com

CONTENTS

3. Facing Life

4. Learning and Growing

5. Coping with Daily Life

6. Walking with God

7. Developing Our Personalities

8. Overcoming Bad Habits

9. Establishing Goals

10. Relating to Other People

11. Developing Social Values

12. Prayers for Special Occasions

13. Prayers for Other People

INTRODUCTION

For many families, daily prayer together is limited to grace before meals. And too often that prayer is just another thing to accomplish, or worse, merely dull, repetitive, and not very meaningful. Most of us have relatively little time spent together with the family. So whether we pray briefly before meals or at another time, what a shame not to try to make it much more meaningful!

We can engage our family prayer-time quite simply—by taking only a few seconds out before our meal to share a short prayer. It will not only draw us closer together as a family but will also plant a bit of life-enchancing wisdom in all of us.

This book contains a collection of very brief, thought-provoking, character-building prayers that can instill important life-enriching concepts in ourselves and in our children.

Since these prayers deal with everyday, family-oriented issues, they might at times also serve as springboards for some very interesting and instructive family discussions during a meal or even during a drive in the car.

The first chapter contains some conventional before-meal prayers, which may be read in addition to a selection from one of the other chapters. And many of these prayers can be read by younger family members, who may respond to the prayer with much more interest as readers than they might if they are only listeners.

May this book be daily spiritual bread for your family's spiritual growth.

ONE

Dinnertime Blessings and Thanksgiving

Asking for a Blessing

We come together to ask you, Lord,
   to bless our food,
      our home,
         and our family.

Appreciating Our Abundance

We join together, Lord, to pray
   for all the people
      who are not fortunate enough
         to have the abundance of food
         that we usually have.
   Bless them, dear God.

Expressing Our Praise

We praise you, Lord, and thank you
   for the food and friendship
      we share with each other today—
      and every day.

Appreciating Our Blessings

Dear Lord, don't let us ever forget
   how blessed and lucky we all are
      to be here
         enjoying this food together.
We thank you, Lord.

Expressing Our Gratitude

We are grateful, Lord,
   that you have blessed us—
      with this wealth of food,
      with this wonderful family,
      and with this safe and secure home.

Staying Connected in Gratitude

As we join hands around the table, Lord,
   bless us all and remind us
      how important it is for us
         to always stay connected—
            in gratitude,
            in caring,
            and in love.

TWO

Appreciating
Home
and
Family

Appreciating Our Family

Remind us, Lord,
   of how lucky we are
      to be part of a loving family.

Thank you for letting us have
   these precious people in our lives.

Bless and help those who don't have
   a family to love and care for them.

Establishing a Loving Home

We ask you to bless our home, Lord.

May each of us always be willing
   to do everything we can
      to make our home
         into a secure and happy place
      where we can give our love and friendship
         to each other—
            and to all who visit us.

Appreciating Each Other

Lord, teach us how to see
   each member of our family
      as a unique, special, and precious person.

Help us learn to appreciate and enjoy
   not only the things we have in common
      but also the differences between us.

May we always go out of our way
   to accept each other just as we are.

Being a Supportive Family

Teach us, Lord,
    how to be a caring and supportive family.

May we always be willing to go out of our way
        to help one another
    whenever any of us is facing a problem.

Teach us how to support,
    encourage, and comfort each other.

And may we never hesitate
    to join together
        in praying for each other.

Expecting Perfection

When we get annoyed
    with each other's faults and imperfections,
        when we get impatient with each other's mistakes,
remind us, Lord, that each day
    everyone in our family has to put up
        with *our* annoying faults and mistakes.

Let us learn how to be nice enough
    to put up with theirs.

How can we expect others to be perfect
    when we are not perfect ourselves?

Cooperating with Each Other

Remind us, Lord,
    that the lack of cooperation in a family
        can make daily living really miserable.

Let us always go out of our way
    to avoid doing anything
        that will make each others' lives
            difficult and unpleasant.

Teach us how to be kind to each other—
    even when we don't especially feel
        like being kind.

Treating Our Family Well

We admit, Lord, that there are times
    when we don't even care
        if we are mean and nasty to our family.

We often treat strangers better
    than we treat our own family.

Let us realize how unfair it is
    to take our frustrations out on them.

Remind us that there will be times
    when we'll need each other's help and friendship.

Let us do our best to build good relationships
    with each and every one in our family.

Being Tolerant

Whenever we're tempted to think
    that someone in our family
        is just too hard to live with—
           and too hard to love—
remind us, Lord,
    that there are times, many times,
        when we, too, are hard to live with
           and hard to love.

Developing Strong Family Ties

Lord, don't let us ever become
    a family that drifts apart.

Teach us, Lord,
    how to truly care for one another.

Let us always be ready and willing
    to share each other's concerns,
    to help with each other's problems,
    to praise each other's achievements,
    and to enjoy each other's friendship.

And as the years go by, let us always remain
    a close-knit, loving, caring group.

Appreciating Our Home

We often forget how lucky we are
  to have a good, secure, and comfortable home.

We thank you, Lord, for giving us
  the privilege of living in this home.

We ask you to bless and help all the people
  who do not have a safe and comfortable home
    to live in.

Doing Our Fair Share

Lord, don't let us upset others
  by constantly putting off doing the jobs
    that we're supposed to do.

Sometimes we're tempted to just sit back
  and wait around for others to do the things
    that ought to be done by us.

Teach us, Lord,
  to always be willing to pitch in
    and pull our fair share of the load.

Making Our Home Pleasant

Remind us, Lord,
  that if we would like our home to be
    a pleasant and enjoyable place
      in which to live,
each of us must do our part
    to make it pleasant and enjoyable.

Resenting Family Rules

Lord, whenever we happen to resent
   our family's rules and restrictions,
let us remind ourselves to be grateful
   that we have someone in our lives
     who cares enough about us to make rules
      that intend to protect us from harm and
      trouble.

Let us remember to be thankful
   that we are so loved and cared for.

Deserving Family Loyalty

Let us realize, Lord,
   that our family is made up of people
     who will always stand by us—
     even when we're crabby and disagreeable.

They may complain about our bad behavior,
   but they usually put up with it—
   and end up giving us their love and support.

Lord, make us worthy of such loyalty.

THREE

Facing Life

Facing the Good and the Bad

Let us realize, Lord,
　　that life is a mixture of many things—
　　of pleasures and pains,
　　　　of triumphs and failures,
　　　　of good times and bad.

Don't let us get so discouraged with the bad
　　that we're not able to look forward hopefully
　　and eagerly to all the times that are good.

Let us realize that life moves in cycles
　　and eventually things usually do get better.

Embracing All of Life

We thank you, Lord,
　　not only for all the nice things that happen each day,
　　but also for the things that are not so nice.

Show us how to embrace
　　　　all that life has to offer—
　　and how to be thankful that our lives
　　　　can be so challenging and interesting.

Choosing to Be Good

Lord,
　　you created us with a will that is free—
　　free to choose to be good or to be bad,
　　　　to be understanding or to be disagreeable,
　　　　to be hardworking or to be lazy,
　　　　to be forgiving or to be vengeful.

Help us to always make the right choices.

Coping With Life

Lord, we know that life isn't easy
    and that it isn't always fair.

Show us how to deal with and accept
    both the hardships and the unfairness of life
        without getting discouraged.

We know that, if we ask,
    you will guide us
        in working our way through
            the tougher parts of life.

Valuing the Right Things

We often think that we'd be really happy
    if we could only get all the things that we want.

Remind us, Lord, that material things
    don't usually bring lasting happiness.

We must do right and act right
    to feel contented and good.

We must love and be loved
    to feel secure and happy.

Valuing Each Day

Lord, may we learn how to greet each new day
    with a positive and cheerful outlook.

Let us view each day as a gift—
    as another chance to accomplish something,
    to help someone,
    to make someone happy.

Counting Our Blessings

Lord, we often allow a few disappointing things
    to make us forget all the good things
        that exist in our lives.

When we're tempted to feel dissatisfied,
    remind us, Lord,
        to sit down and count our blessings.

Let us always be aware
    of just how blessed and lucky we are.

Developing a Sense of Humor

We thank you, Lord, for giving us
    the precious gift of laughter.

Let us remember to use this gift
    to brighten our own lives
        and those of our family and friends.

Teach us, Lord, how to develop
    a good sense of humor.

Doing Our Best

Remind us, Lord,
    that the more we put into life,
        the more we'll get out of it.

May we always choose to study hard
    and do our very best
        to make our lives a success.

And give us the ability to make ourselves
    into individuals we can be proud of.

Choosing Our Attitudes

Remind us, Lord, that we have the power
    to choose our attitudes toward life.

We can choose
    to be satisfied or dissatisfied,
    to be contented or discontented.

It's up to us to choose
    whether we want to live our lives cheerfully
    or with a sad and gloomy outlook.

Facing Our Challenges

O Lord,
    we can choose to face life's challenges
        with either a sense of dread
        or a sense of adventure.

Help us to approach our challenges
        eagerly and confidently—
    knowing and trusting
        that you will always be at our side,
            ready and willing to help us.

Being Positive

Remind us, Lord, that we can face
    the discouraging things that happen in life
        with a negative, self-pitying attitude
        or with a positive, accepting,
            and hopeful attitude.

When we are tempted to feel sorry for ourselves,
    give us the courage to remember
        that facing life with a positive attitude
            makes our lives a lot easier.

Developing a Spirit of Adventure

Lord, teach us how to live each day
    with a spirit of adventure, curiosity, and wonder.

Let us constantly seek out
    new things to learn,
        new people to meet,
            and new and interesting things to do.

Help us to accept, Lord,
    that if our lives become dull and boring,
        it's because we allow them
            to become dull and boring.

Inspire us to take responsibility
    for living our lives to the full.

Coping With Failure

Teach us, Lord,
 that we don't have to feel so discouraged
  when we meet with an occasional failure—
 especially if we've done our best to succeed.

After all, everyone fails at times.

Show us, Lord, how to view a failure
 not as a final unfixable tragedy
 but rather as just another chance
  to learn a new and different way
   to accomplish something.

FOUR

Learning
and
Growing

Being Open to Learning

We are often unwilling
    to listen to the views of other people—
especially if they don't agree with our views.

Lord, may we not be so arrogant
    and narrow-minded as to believe
        that our way of thinking and doing things
            is always the best way.

Instead, may we be such good listeners
    that we discover something new and helpful
        from listening to the views of others,
            especially when we don't agree.

Accepting Responsibility for Our Actions

Lord,
    it's so easy to blame others
        for some wrong that we do.

Lead us instead to take
    full responsibility for all of our actions.

If anyone manages
    to talk us into doing something wrong,
        we are the ones who choose
    to allow them to talk us into it—
        so we are still responsible.

Show us the beauty of acting
    only in ways that represent our very best.

Dealing With Disappointments

Lord, help us to understand
    that disappointments are just a normal part of life—
        everyone's life.

Don't let us fall into the trap
    of allowing ourselves to get discouraged
        and depressed over disappointing events.

Give us the ability to quickly put
    our disappointments behind us
        and pay more attention to the many good things
        that happen each day.

Learning Respect

Lord, don't let us be tempted
    to be rude and nasty to others.

May we always go out of our way
    to be polite and respectful.

Remind us
    that we will deserve to get respect
    only when we are willing to give respect.

Learning to Persevere

Let us always remember, Lord,
    that a person is not a failure
        unless that person is too afraid,
        too discouraged,
        or too lazy to keep on trying.

Lord, don't let us be tempted to give up easily.

Learning from Mistakes

Lord, we know that each defeat,
    each failure,
        each mistake we make
            contains some lesson for us.

Help us learn
    not only how to recognize the lesson
    but also how to make it a part of our lives.

Developing Good Sportsmanship

Help us, Lord,
    to be good sports in everything we do.

When we are winners,
    let us win because we've done our best
        and have dealt fairly with others.

And when we lose,
    let us lose graciously
        and without feeling sorry for ourselves.

Accepting Life As It Is

Teach us how to accept life as it is.

Let us learn to be more at peace
        with whatever happens each day
    and not waste our time vainly wishing
        for things to be different.

Teach us how to be able
    to find something good in everything
        that happens to come our way.

Learning to Forgive

Lord, help us to be kind enough
    to immediately accept the apologies
        that others offer us.

And let us also be ready and willing
    to let go of any resentments we may feel.

Help us to let go
    of any spiteful or vengeful feelings.

May we be mature enough
    to forgive others as you forgive us.

Facing Difficulties

Let us realize, Lord,
    that to enjoy a fulfilling life,
        we must accept all of it—
    not only its pleasures and successes
    but also its problems and disappointments.

Let us learn how to accept and live with
    both the tough and the easy parts of life.

Remind us that we often learn more
    and become stronger and more confident
        from facing the tougher things in life.

Learning How to Disagree

Because we are all so different
   with different ideas and opinions,
      we often disagree with one another.

Teach us, Lord, how to disagree
   without hurting, insulting,
      or ridiculing each other.

Inspire us to state our ideas respectfully,
   to listen just as respectfully to others,
      and to do the work that can result
         in a meeting of hearts and minds.

Developing Honesty

Lord, help us to be truthful
   in all that we say and do.

May we never be willing
   to be deceitful and dishonest.

Lying often requires more lying
   to cover up our dishonesty.

It also makes others distrust us.

Give us the grace to decide
      to be truthful and trustworthy people.

Learning to Apologize

Lord, it's often very hard for us
    to apologize, so we keep putting it off.

Let us realize that the longer we wait,
    the more time there is
        for bad feelings to build up.

Don't let us ever be so stubborn
    that we are unable to say we're sorry
        quickly and sincerely.

Listening to Advice

Lord, we often feel angry and resentful
    when someone tries to give us advice—
        especially when someone older tries to advise us.

Let us realize that, when people give advice,
    they usually wish to be helpful,
        rather than critical.

Let us learn to be open to their suggestions,
    for they often want to save us
        from making mistakes that they made.

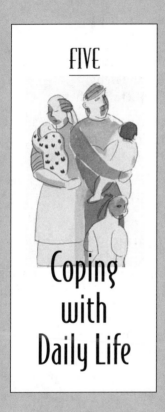

FIVE

Coping with Daily Life

Breaking Cycles of Frustration

Lord, we often get very upset
    with people who nag us.

When we do, remind us
    to stop and ask ourselves
        if we have the right
            to get upset with them.

If we haven't done what we ought to do,
    show us that our behavior
        makes the nagging possible.

Give us the sense of fairness and the kindness
    to do what we ought to do.

Searching for Happiness

We often think that we'll finally be happy
    if only things happen the way we want them to.

Lord, show us that it's not just
    the things that happen in our lives
        that make us sad or happy.

It's how well we accept and respond
    to all that happens.

Teach us how to respond
    in a more accepting and positive manner.

Dealing with Problems

Let us always remember, Lord,
    that we can choose to face our problems
        with worry and despair
        or with hope and confidence.

Remind us that worry never accomplishes much.
    It simply wears us down.

Teach us, Lord, how to face our problems
    with a positive attitude
        and faith in your help.

Respecting Property

Lord, remind us to always respect
    the possessions and property of others.

Don't let us ever be tempted
    to take or to destroy anything
        that belongs to someone else.

May we care for the possessions of others
    as we would like others to care for ours.

Learning How to Criticize

Teach us, Lord,
    how to give criticism and advice
        without hurting, offending,
            or ridiculing others.

We promise to make sure that our criticism
    is always constructive and kind
        rather than destructive and mean.

Expressing Appreciation

Lord, don't let us ever
    become so self-centered and ungrateful
        that we fail to show our appreciation
            for all that others do for us.

Our parents, teachers, family, and friends
    do a lot to make our lives better.

Let us always make it a point
    to openly express our thanks,
        our praise, and our appreciation.

Saying "No" to Drugs

Lord, may we never be tempted to think
    that alcohol and drugs are all right to use.

We are aware of how harmful
        these addictive substances are—
    not only harmful
        to our own bodies and minds,
    but also to all the people who may be hurt
        by the impaired and reckless behavior
            these drugs can cause in us.

Help us to always act with love and consideration
    for ourselves and others.

Facing Unpleasant Things

Lord, there are some things in life
that are really unpleasant to do.

We all have to take turns
doing jobs that we don't especially like to do.

Remind us, Lord, that
we can't always do *only* the things
that we like to do.

Playing Fairly

Lord, let us always remember to be good sports
and play fairly in all our competitions.

May we never let our abilities go to our heads
and cause us to compete for our own glory
instead of the good of our team.

And don't let us ever be guilty of putting down
those who are not as good as we are.

Teach us to be fair
and unconceited competitors.

Going Along With the Crowd

We're often tempted to just go along with the crowd,
even when we know—deep in our hearts—
that what they're doing is wrong.

Lord, give us the wisdom and strength we need
not only to resist following their lead,
but to openly disapprove
of behavior that is wrong and irresponsible.

Avoiding Regrets

There are times, Lord, when we draw back
    from facing new experiences and challenges.

Give us the courage and confidence we need
    to face these experiences more willingly.

May we never end up regretting
    that we missed an opportunity
        to do something worthwhile.

Instead, may we embrace even serious challenges
    by trusting in you to help and guide us.

Taking Frustrations Out on Others

When we feel bad, Lord,
    we often want to make others feel bad too.

Help us to avoid taking our crabbiness
    and frustrations out on those we love—
        those who are closest to us.

Let us realize how unfair this is.

Teach us how to be nicer to each other—
    even when we don't happen
        to feel like being nice.

Building Good Relationships

Lord, give us the good grace
    not to waste our time
        in petty arguments and disagreements.

We accomplish a lot more
    by using positive means
        to build good and enjoyable relationships.
        Show us the right way to love
            each person we encounter today.

Having Our Own Way

Let us realize, Lord,
    that we can't always have our own way.

Each of us has different points of view,
    different likes and dislikes,
        and different ways of doing things.

Let us learn to respect the ways of others
    and always be willing
        to meet others halfway.

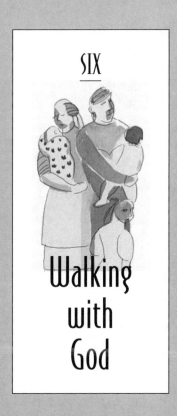

SIX

Walking
with
God

Walking with You, Lord

Show us
how to always walk with you, Lord—
step by step, day by day.

Take our hands
and lead us in the direction
you want us to take.

Show us how we can serve you
and draw closer to you each day.

Forgetting About You, Lord

Lord, when things go wrong,
we immediately turn to you for help.

But when everything's going right
and we're enjoying ourselves,
we often forget all about you.

Forgive us, Lord, for all the times
we fail to think of you
and talk to you.

Sharing Our Days

Teach us, Lord, how to share
every part of our lives with you.

Be with us during each part of our day—
at home, at school, at our jobs,
during the hours we spend
with family and friends.

Lord, be with us always and everywhere.

Accepting Your Will

In our prayers, Lord,
    we keep saying, "Thy will be done."

However, we get terribly upset
    when your will doesn't agree with our wishes.

It seems that what we really want
    is for things to always go our way.

Help us, Lord, to accept
    whatever you think is best for us.

Serving You, Lord

Lord, show us how we can make
    each job we do
        each project we undertake
            each kindness we perform for others
    into a prayer—
        a prayer that is worthy
            to be offered up to you.

Having You in Our Lives

Thank you, Lord, for always being at our sides
    to listen to us
        to help us
            to guide us
                and to love us.

Thank you for staying near us when we need you.
    We're so blessed to have you in our lives.

Learning How to Pray

Dear Lord, teach us how to pray.

Instead of constantly praying
    for things to happen the way we want them to,
we can learn to pray for the wisdom,
    the strength, and the courage we need
        to accept and live with whatever happens
            in our lives each day.

Disappointing You, Lord

Do we disappoint you, Lord,
    when we fail to do the things
        that we ought to do?

Do we make you sad
    when we don't treat others
        as well as we should?

We're sorry, Lord, for disappointing you.

We'll try harder to do what's right.

Forgetting to Be Thankful

Our prayers are often
    like letters to Santa Claus, Lord.

At times they're nothing more than long lists
    of what we want from you.

But why should you give us all that we ask for,
    when we often forget to be thankful
        for what we already have?

Needing You, Lord

There are times, Lord,
   when we make our lives harder
      by making the wrong decisions.

And we often do so
   because we forget to pray
      and ask for your guidance.

Why do we keep forgetting that we need
   your help to live our lives wisely?

Lord, make us constantly aware
   of just how much we need you.

Facing Difficulties

Lord, we so often lack courage
   when it comes to dealing with
      the difficult and frightening things in life.

And instead of immediately
   turning to you for help,
      we react with fear and discouragement.

Teach us, Lord, how to keep our spirits up
   and have faith that, with you beside us,
      we can successfully face
         even the tough and scary things in our lives.

Appreciating Your World

We thank you, Lord,
    for all the beautiful things
        you have put on this earth of ours—
        the forests and flowers
        the mountains and valleys
        the oceans and streams
        the stars and the sunsets.

You created them all
    for our pleasure and enjoyment.

You are a good and loving God.

Doing What's Right

Lord, make us
    not only wise enough
        to know what is right
    but also strong enough
        to do what is right.

Silencing Our Noisy World

Lord, it seems that our television sets,
    stereos, and radios are constantly blaring.

How can we ever hear your voice and your guidance
    when we continuously surround ourselves
        with so much noise?

Remind us to take some time each day
    to shut off the noise of our world for a while
        so we can speak and listen to you.

SEVEN

Developing
Our
Personalities

Choosing Our Personality

Remind us, Lord, that we can't
blame others for the way we are.

We are the ones—the *only* ones—
who can decide how we want to act.

We are the only ones who can change
the things that need to be changed
so we can become the kind of people
that we want to be.

Knowing What's Important

Lord, help us to keep our priorities straight
and never lose sight
of what's really important in life—
what we make of ourselves,
what we accomplish,
our relationships with others,
and our relationship with you, Lord.

Feeling Worthy

Lord, there are times when we feel
unimportant, unworthy, and totally inadequate.

When we feel this way, please step in
and restore our self-confidence.

Lift our spirits, Lord,
and help us to feel good about ourselves.

Love us when we find it hard
to love ourselves.

Dealing with Our Faults

Remind us, Lord, that we possess the power
    to either hold on to our faults
        or to ask for your grace
        to lessen them or get rid of them.

We often try to make excuses for our faults,
    and we don't even try to change our behavior.

Let us realize
    that you can help us change hurtful behavior
        and transform our hearts—
    but only if we stop excusing our faults
        and ask you to help us.

Feeling Special

Whenever we feel dissatisfied with ourselves,
whenever we find it difficult to love ourselves,
    remind us, Lord,
        that you created us and love us
            just the way we are.

Show us how to see ourselves
    as special and precious
        in your sight.

Thank you, Lord, for loving us
        as much as you do,
        and so much more than we can imagine.

Overcoming Discouragement

Lord, don't let us get discouraged
     when we feel that we're not doing well
          in whatever we're trying to accomplish.

Give us the strength and determination we need
     to just work a little harder.

And give us the confidence we need
     to believe in ourselves
          and in our eventual success.

Facing Our Imperfections

Lord, we're often very quick to see
     the faults in other people,
          but very slow to notice our own faults.

Let us be honest enough to see ourselves
     as we really are—a mixture of good and bad—
          just like the people we often criticize.

Teach us, Lord, to be less critical of others.

Developing an Important Talent

Whenever we're tempted to think
     that we have absolutely no talents,

remind us, Lord, that each and every one of us
     has the talent to be a friend—
          to give help, comfort, and love to others.

We all have the talent
     to enrich the lives of other people
          with our friendship and support.

Changing Our Attitudes

Lord, let us realize that,
   although we can't usually change
      the things that happen in life,
   we can always change the attitudes
      with which we face life.

Let us learn how to choose attitudes
   that will make our lives—
      and the lives of those who are close to us—
         easier and more enjoyable.

Toughing It Out

When our lives get unpleasant and tough,
   give us the wisdom to let go of resentment.

Let us remember, Lord,
   that it's the tough and abrasive things in life
      that can best smooth out and polish
         the rough edges of our personalities.

Remind us that it's often
      the tough things in life
            that make us strong.

Help Us Do Right

Lord, we don't always have the courage
   or the desire to do what we know is right.

We ask you, Lord, to pull us back
      when we go wrong
   and push us forward
      when we're too afraid,
         too lazy,
            or too stubborn
      to do what's right.

Taking Care of Our Bodies

Lord, you have given us remarkable bodies.

Remind us that we have an obligation
   to take care of them
      and keep them strong and healthy.

May we have the good sense never to do anything
      or indulge in anything
   that will harm or damage our bodies.

May we do as good a job of caring for our bodies
   as you would do.

Being Self-Centered

Lord, don't let us become people
   who are selfish and self-centered.

At times, we just don't care how others feel
   as long as we can do what we want
      and feel contented and satisfied.

Let us learn to be
   more aware of and concerned about
      the feelings and happiness of others.

Storing Good Memories

Lord, each day we experience things
   that will become memories in our future.

Let us always make sure
   that we're able to store memories
      that are enjoyable and good,
      not hurtful or shameful.

Let us be able to fill our lives
   with memories that we can all treasure.

EIGHT

Overcoming
Bad Habits

Being Dissatisfied

Lord, we're often guilty of feeling dissatisfied
and complaining about things we don't like.

Let us realize that no one likes to listen
to a sulking, whining complainer.

Help us to get rid of this annoyingly bad habit
and to become more satisfied
more contented
and much more likeable.

Coping with Worry

Lord, we often waste so much time and energy
regretting the past and worrying about the future
that we don't have enough strength
to live well in the present.

Teach us, Lord, how to live one day at a time.

Getting Rid of Self-Pity

Sometimes it's really comforting
to just sit back and feel sorry for ourselves.

Lord, help us to see
what a waste of time it is to
submerge ourselves in a pool of self-pity.

It is a crippling emotion that can keep us
from living an enjoyable life.

May we never allow ourselves
to get caught in its trap.

Blaming Others for Our Failures

Lord, don't let us be tempted
   to blame others for our failures.

We can fool ourselves into believing
      that we didn't succeed
   because we weren't taught right
   or because we weren't given
      the advantages that others have.

We can go on excusing ourselves
   or we can make up our minds to work harder.

Help us, Lord, to make the right choice.

Envying the Lives of Others

Lord, we sometimes envy other people
   because we think
      that they're luckier and happier than we are.

Let us realize that everyone's life
   is filled with both good and bad.

Everyone has problems to deal with
   even though they aren't always obvious.

Let us learn to accept—and even be grateful—
   for our own problems.

And let us be thankful that we don't have to face
   some of the terrible problems that others must face.

Holding On to Anger

Lord, when something happens to make us angry,
    we can choose to either stay angry
        or to let go of our angry feelings.

Remind us, Lord, that anger
    is more damaging to us than it is
        to those with whom we are angry.

Teach us how to let go
    of this energy-draining emotion.

Curtailing Gossip

When we hear some gossip about someone, Lord,
    we often can't wait to pass it on to others.

Let us realize how cruel and destructive it is
    to speak unkindly about other people.

We certainly wouldn't like others to talk about us.

Help us, Lord, to be kind enough
    not to gossip about others.

Resisting the Temptation to Cheat

Lord, don't let us ever be tempted
    to be dishonest enough to cheat.

We sometimes think that it's all right to cheat
    either because we see others do it
        or because it's just the easier thing to do.

Let us realize that when we choose to cheat
    we are usually cheating and hurting ourselves.

Complaining About Chores

Lord, we often complain about
    all the household chores we have to do.

But when we stop to think
    of all the people who are poor and homeless,
    we are grateful, Lord, that we have
        floors to sweep, rugs to vacuum,
        tables to dust, and dishes to wash.

Remind us not to complain so much.

Using Bad Language

Lord, some people think it's cool
    to use bad language and make remarks
        that are coarse and obscene.

Let us realize how childish
        and unintelligent this is.

Don't let us be drawn into acting
    so immaturely and stupidly.

Being Boastful

There are times, Lord, when we're tempted to think
    that we're better and more talented than others.

Let us remember that any talents we possess
    are gifts that you have chosen to give us.

Remind us that they were given
    not to make us boastful and smug
    but to make us more able to help and serve others.

Winning Arguments

Lord, we're often so addicted to being right
    that, when we get into an argument,
      we're usually determined to win it at any cost.

Remind us, Lord,
    it's not as important to win an argument
      as it is to learn something from it.

Getting Rid of Jealousy

Lord, don't let us ever be jealous
    of the good fortune of others.

Grant us the ability to be genuinely pleased
    when something nice happens to other people.

And give us the grace to be able to show them
    how happy we are for them.

Dreading Tomorrow

We tend to fret about
    all the "what-ifs" in our lives.

Lord, don't let us constantly worry
    about what tomorrow may bring.

Remind us that many of the things we dread
    end up never really happening.

Let us learn to simply trust in your help
    and always firmly believe that you will
      give us the strength to deal with tomorrow
        when tomorrow finally comes.

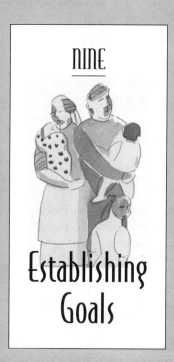

NINE

Establishing Goals

Preparing for Our Life's Work

Lord, help us to realize how important it is
    to prepare ourselves well
        for the future jobs in our lives.

Let us always do our best
    to keep our minds educated,
    our attitudes positive,
    and our faith in ourselves and in you
        strong and firm.

Fulfilling Our Mission

Lord, we may never do great things
    and become famous on this earth,
but we know that each one of us
    has a special mission to accomplish in life.

Show each of us what we can do
    to make our corner of the world
        a little nicer place in which to live.

Setting Goals

Lord, don't let us be tempted
    to just go drifting aimlessly through life—
        through our studies, our jobs, our chores—
    always taking the easy way out.

Give us the determination we need
    to set specific goals for ourselves.

And give us the energy we need
    to work hard to achieve those goals.

Making Our Lives Meaningful

Lord, we know that we have not been placed
    on this earth merely to take up space.

Remind us that you hold us responsible
    for living a life
        that is useful and meaningful.

Let us always remember that we are all here
    to share our talents and abilities with each other—
        to help, to support, and to love each other,
        and to know, to serve, and to love you,
            our Lord and Creator.

Developing Our Talents

Let us understand, Lord,
    that the talents you've given us
        don't usually come to us fully developed.

It's up to us to do our best
    to develop them and to use them
        wisely and well.

We ask you for the perseverance
    to develop and use our talents
        for our own good and that of others.

Discovering the Right Path

Lord, we're often very confused and uncertain
   about what our special job in life should be.

Lead us in the direction you want us to go.

Show us how to trust you
   and be open to your guidance.

May we do everything we can to discover
   how we can best serve you
      and the people in our lives.

Show us what we can do to make
   our world a better and happier place.

Feeling Inadequate

Teach us, Lord, not to waste our time
   being jealous of what other people can do.

Let us learn to concentrate instead
   on discovering and developing
      the unique and special talents
         that you have chosen to give us.

Remind us, Lord, that if we spend less time
   feeling bad about the things we can't do,
      we'll have more time
to develop the things we can.

Taking Advantage of Opportunities

Keep reminding us, Lord, that it's our own fault
    if we don't take advantage of opportunities
        that are presented to us.

We have the power to make our lives
    either productive and fulfilling
        or mediocre and disappointing.

Help us to always make the right choices.

Fullfilling Our Dreams

Lord, don't let us ever be tempted
    to let go of the dreams that we have.

There are times
    when we get discouraged and lose hope
    and times when we get lazy
        and want to give up.

Help us, Lord,
    to be willing to study and work hard
    to make our lives meaningful and enjoyable.

Needing Your Help

Whenever we begin to feel overwhelmed
    and burdened by our mission in life,
remind us, Lord, that you never expected us
    to achieve our life's goals
        without your help and guidance.

We trust that you will stay near us, Lord,
    and always help us.

TEN

Relating
to
Other People

Seeing Good in Others

Lord, let us learn to see
  the good in other people
    rather than the bad.

Give us the ability to focus on
  their strengths rather than their faults.

Let us realize that
  every person has something good inside.

And it's up to us to find it.

Taking Care of Each Other

There are times, Lord, when we're so absorbed
    in our own selfish concerns
  that we're completely unaware
    of the needs of others.

Give us the ability to notice
  when other people need our help and support.

Teach us how to really take care of one another.

Making Fun of Others

There are times, Lord, when it seems
  that we actually enjoy teasing
    and making fun of others.

Let us realize how mean and unkind
  it is to laugh at others.

Teach us, Lord, to treat others
  as we would like them to treat us.

Influencing Other People

Lord, grant that we may always be
    a good influence on the people
        that we meet each day in our lives.

Don't let us ever be responsible
    for prompting others to be mean, angry,
        destructive, or immoral.

May each person we meet
    become better for having known us.

Being a Good Friend

There are times, Lord,
    when we get annoyed with our friends
        and become very critical and judgmental.

Let us learn to accept our friends as they are
    and not expect them to be perfect.

Teach us to always be loyal, understanding,
    forgiving, and loving.

And help us realize how lucky we are
    to have good friends in our lives.

Making Others Feel Good

Help us, Lord, to avoid saying or doing things
    that will make others feel hurt,
        humiliated, or discouraged.

Give us the ability
    to make other people
        feel important, happy, and good.

Helping Someone

We're sorry, Lord, for all the times
   we have failed to help someone.

There are times when we hesitate too long
   to step forward and offer our help and support—
      and the opportunity passes.

We'll try to be more aware of the needs of others
   and do our best to help as quickly as possible.

Being More Loving

Lord, some people are so terribly annoying!
   They're not only hard to understand
      but also hard to love.

Whenever we're tempted to be unkind to such people,
   remind us, Lord, that there are times
      when we, too, are annoying,
         hard to understand,
         and hard to love.

Being Kind to Others

There are times, Lord,
   when we feel mean and disagreeable
      and really eager to start an argument.

Teach us to refrain from speaking angry words
   and inspire us to react to others with more
      kindness.

Remind us to take time out
   when we're feeling angry.

Loving the Unlovable

Teach us, Lord, to be kind to people
who are often annoying and irritating.

Let us realize that their annoying behavior
may be caused by personal problems
that they find hard to deal with.

Let us learn to be more patient,
more understanding, and more loving
to those who are not very lovable.

Remind us that it's often the most unlovable people
who need the most love.

Choosing Good Friends

Lord, let us always be both wise
and cautious in choosing our friends.

May we never choose as friends
people who are reckless and irresponsible
people who influence us to do things
contrary to our values.

Send us friends who are kind and loyal,
who enjoy doing the good things we enjoy, too.

And may we be deserving of such friends.

Being Supportive

Lord, let us be able to notice
   when someone needs a comforting hug,
      a word of praise,
         or a pat on the back.

Remind us to always be available
   to give others the encouragement,
      comfort, and support they need.

Help us remember to spend
   at least a few moments each day
      making someone a little happier.

Accepting People Who Are Different

Lord, it's so easy to like people
   who think the way we do,
      act the way we do,
         and always agree with us.

Let us learn to accept and respect those
   who have different ideas than we have.

Let us learn to be more tolerant open-minded,
   and loving.

Remind us that we can't really know
   why others are as they are
      and act as they do
   unless we have walked for a while
      in their shoes.

ELEVEN

Developing
Social Values

Respecting Authority

Lord, remind us to always show respect for authority—
   at home, at school, and in our community.

Don't let us ever be tempted
   to be disruptive, disrespectful,
      or unfairly critical of those
         who are trying to keep order in our world.

Let us always set a good example for others to follow.

Keeping Our World Beautiful

Lord, you have entrusted us
   with a world that has great beauty.

But we don't always take good care
   of what you have given us.

Remind us to do a better job.

Making Our World Better

Let us remember, Lord,
   that we each possess the ability
      to make this world of ours better.

Let us learn to always look for a chance
   to perform some little act of kindness
      for our friends and neighbors
      for acquaintances
      and even for strangers.

Let us always strive to make
   the lives of others easier and more pleasant.

Doing For Others

Remind us, Lord,
    that the happiest, the most contented people
        are usually those who are willing
            to share their time, their support,
                and their friendship with others.

Let us also remember, Lord,
    that anything we do for others,
        we do for you.

Promoting Good Values

Lord, it's so hard not to notice
    all the violence and immorality
        in our media,
        our games, and our music.

Give us the wisdom we need
    to avoid being influenced
        by corrupt views and ideas.

Teach us not only to hold firmly to our values
    but also to become active in influencing others
        to promote values that are good.

Thinking of Others

Keep reminding us, Lord,
    that if we spend more time
        being concerned about other people,
    there will be less time left
        to worry about ourselves.

Speaking Up for Beliefs

Lord, give us the courage
   to stand up for what we believe in.

May we never be intimidated
   into keeping quiet about
      the things we believe in—
   even if others disagree with us
      or even try to belittle us.

Reaching Out to Others

Let us realize, Lord,
   that all the blessings and privileges we enjoy
      bring with them a responsibility—
   a responsibility to reach out and help others
      who are not as fortunate as we are.

Preventing Hatred

Lord, don't let us ever be tempted
   to look down on or to be mean to people
      who we feel are odd or unpopular.

Let us realize that when people are treated badly,
   they sometimes respond with anger and violence.

Don't let us ever be guilty of promoting
   hatred and violence in our world
      by being cruel to others.

Remind us that everyone is your child
   and deserves to be treated with kindness.

Avoiding Prejudice

Lord, remove from us all ignorance of
and prejudice against
people of other cultures.

May we not be so arrogant
that we think we are better than others.

We promise to imitate your example
by being not only respectful and kind
to all people
but also courageous enough to speak up
when we notice that others
are being treated cruelly or unfairly.

TWELVE

Prayers
for
Special
Occasions

New Year's Day

As we begin a brand-new year,
we ask you for your blessings, Lord.

Let this year be filled with
good health, peace, joy, and achievements.

Give us the strength we need
to live through both the good and the bad times.

And let our love for each other
and our faith in you
grow stronger with each passing day.

Easter

We feel so fortunate to be able
to come together today
to celebrate the joyous feast of Easter.

We thank you, Lord,
for suffering and dying for our sins
and for opening heaven to us.

Let us celebrate the joy
of your Resurrection
today and every day.

Thanksgiving

Lord, we come together today to give you thanks
for the many blessings you have granted us—
for the food we enjoy each day,
for the home we live in,
for our precious family and friends.

In our hearts and through our actions,
make a way for help to come to those
who are not as fortunate as we are.

Christmas

We join our hands today
in celebration of your birthday, Lord.

We thank you for coming to our earthly home
to teach us how to live.

May we keep the spirit of Christmas
alive throughout the coming year
by sharing our love and concern
with all the people in our lives.

Birthday

Lord, we come together today to ask you
   to bless (N.) on his/her birthday.

We feel so fortunate that we have (N.)
   in our family.

Shower your blessings upon him/her,
   and give him/her the strength, the wisdom
      and the confidence he/she needs
   to face all the challenges
      that this year will bring.

May it be a year filled with joy.

Parents' Anniversary

We ask you, Lord, to bless us all
   on this, the birthday of our family.

We thank you for the many blessings
   you have granted us
      and for all the happy times
         we have shared together.

Let us continue to grow
   in our love for one another
      and let the coming year be blessed
         with health, happiness, and success.

In Time of Trouble

Lord, you have said that whenever we agree
about anything we pray for,
it will be done for us by your Father in heaven.

For where we come together in your name,
you are here with us.

Lord, we come together today as a family
to join in prayer and ask for your help
in this time of trouble.

Dear Lord, comfort us, guide us, help us,
and bring peace and joy back into our lives.

Please give us what we truly need.

An Accomplishment

Lord, we are so proud of (N.),
whose accomplishment we are celebrating today.

Thank you for helping him/her
to achieve his/her goal.

Bless him/her and give him/her the wisdom
to continue to do well in life.

Dear Lord, let his/her accomplishment serve
as an inspiration for us all to work hard
to attain our dreams and goals.

In Time of Illness

We ask you, Lord,
   to comfort and bless (N.), who is sick.

Please help (N.) to be
   strong enough and patient enough
      to be able to get through
         the discomfort and pain of this illness.

And we pray, Lord,
   that you grant him/her
      a good and speedy recovery.

A Family Gathering

We have come together today, Lord,
   to celebrate the presence of our relatives.

We thank you, Lord,
   for the chance to spend some time
      with this precious family of ours.

Bring joy and blessings to all who are here,
   and let us always remain
      loyal, caring, and loving friends.

THIRTEEN

Prayers
for
Other
People

For People Who Are Lonely

Lord, we're so lucky to have
   a good family and good friends.

Bless and help all the people
   who are alone and lonely
     and have no one to care about them.

Bless and help all those
   who have no one to pray for them.

For People Who Are Poor

Lord, we often ask you to help all the people
   who are living in poverty.

But why are we asking you to help them,
   when you have placed us on this earth
     to do what we can to share our gifts
      and our advantages with others?

Show us what we can do to make the lives
   of those who are poor easier and better.

For Troubled Families

Dear Lord, help the families
   that are being torn apart
     by arguments and abuse.

Help those who find it impossible
   to live together peacefully.

Lord, give us the grace to do everything we can
   to live in harmony with one another.

For Those Who Are Sick

Lord, we ask you to give strength and comfort
    to all the people who are sick and suffering,
    especially to the small children who are ill.

Take away their fears and their pain, Lord,
    and bring comfort and healing to them.

For Abused Young People

Lord, help all the young people
    who are being abused and battered.

Help those who are forced to leave their homes
    because of unsafe and loveless circumstances.

Let them be able to find the help,
    the support, and the love they need.

And remind us, Lord, to be grateful
    for all the love we receive each day.

For Struggling Young People

Lord, help all those young people
    who are confused, misguided, or struggling—
    who are involved in things
        that are harmful and wrong.

Help them to find their way
    to someone or someplace
        where they can receive
the guidance and love they need.

And help them, Lord, to find their way
    back to you, their loving God.

For Mentally Challenged People

Lord, help all those special people
who were not blessed with the mental abilities
with which we were blessed.

Don't let us ever be tempted to make fun of them.

Let us be able to help make their lives easier
by being kind, encouraging, and friendly.

And always help us to be open
to what they can teach us.

For Elderly People

We're so lucky to be basically strong and healthy.

Lord, bless and help the many people
who are old and frail,
who are no longer able to cope with living
as easily as we can.

Show us what we can do to help
make their lives easier and more enjoyable.

For People with Disabilities

Lord, bless and help all the people
who are physically disabled.

We usually take our able bodies for granted
and never give a thought to how difficult
life is for those who can't do
all that we enjoy doing each day.

Lord, give people what they need to face
their daily challenges.

For People in War-torn Countries

Lord, bless and help all the people
    who live in war-torn countries.

Help those who are living in fear—
    who are starving, suffering injuries,
    or losing their homes and their loved ones.

We are humbled and grateful, Lord,
    that you have given us the privilege
        of living in a nation that values freedom and
            peace.

Other titles of interest...

Prayers for Married Couples
Renee Bartkowski

More than 75 prayers that express the hopes, concerns, and dreams of today's married couples.

(#55775) $5.95

Prayers for Parents
Renee Bartkowski

A guidebook packed with more than 60 prayers that help parents pass on Christian wisdom to their children.

(#55785) $5.95

Blessings of the Table
Mealtime Prayers Throughout the Year
Br. Victor-Antoine d'Avila-Latourrette

A book of seasonal and special-occasion table blessings for adults and children. Based on the daily and seasonal rhythm of the liturgy, with a separate monthly calendar of feasts and memorials of saints, it is inspired by the Catholic tradition but has an appeal that transcends denominational boundaries.

(#16405) $14.95

Order from your local bookstore or write to:
Liguori Publications
One Liguori Drive, Liguori, MO 63057-9999
Please add 15% to your total for shipping and handling
($3.50 minimum, $15 maximum).
For faster service, call toll-free 1-800-325-9521.
Please have your credit card ready.